The Beginner's Creative Real Estate Investing Course

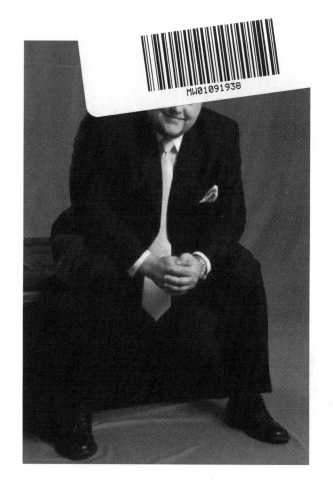

For Flipping Houses

By Zack Childress

www.REISuccessAcademy.net

Table of Contents

Don't Forget to Claim Your Free Bonus That Came with this Book

My Co-Wholesaling Blueprint ($197.00 Value)

The Step by Step Process to Make $5000 in 7 Days

Without any Experience, Cash, or Credit

Download at:

www.Co-Wholesaling.com/ebookbonus

Introduction

The first thing I would like to say is **congratulations**! You have definitely made a great decision to invest in your future and to really take your business to a whole new level.

Understand this: every successful person in life has had a mentor, a coach, or an advisor, consultant, or someone to help with the understanding of proper business models and practices. I am honored that you have elected to have me guide you in the initial stages towards your new way of living!

When examining your business model, sometimes it is very challenging to determine what is not working to the full potential because you are so deeply involved in the day-to-day obligations of being a successful real estate investor.

You are figuratively blinded to your own successes and shortcomings due to your preoccupation in the grind and the monotony of all the daily details. You need a trustworthy guide to channel your focus and direct you in the ways of successful investing practices.

Trust me, I know. There are plenty negative experiences and setbacks I had to go through on my own to reach this level of knowledge and success in real estate investing. Fortunately, you have it a bit easier because of the expertise I am sharing with you.

As you get started with this step-by-step roadmap, you will see that your wildest expectations are going to be exceeded.

I know with certainty that understanding the order of operations is one of the biggest challenges facing most investors.

However, The Beginner's Creative Real Estate Investing Course is a program similar to the old fashioned, "paint-by-numbers' activities. I have created this book so that you will have a guide that will teach you exactly what to do and in which order.

I've laid this book out in such a way that you will learn and complete a constructive income producing company. If you are truly invested in your education, then you will attentively work through each step of this training program.

It will be very important that you follow each chapter in proper succession and implement what we teach you.

Your effort will make this knowledge easier to grasp and more rewarding in the end. This is essentially a business program, similar to any business class at a university.

I am confident that I can help you get your real estate investing business off the ground. Follow this path and you will achieve the success you've been looking for.

As you move through this book of training, I want you to feel empowered. Long before you complete the final lessons, you will realize that this can be achieved.

This caliber of success is possible for you, too! There is nothing more fulfilling than accomplishing a goal that you've been striving to reach. I fully believe your dream will be reached if you apply yourself and work diligently.

Now, let me go ahead and break into what I call, **"The Mindset of Being Successful."**

This is the willingness to know that you can achieve anything that is absolutely possible. You can never be successful until you believe it "upstairs" first. You can never accomplish a long-term endeavor unless you mentally envision your own triumph.

This important pre-requisite may require a reprogramming of your mindset, almost to the point of having a childlike faith and innocence to move forward.

Do not let your passion and conviction that this is going to work be worn down by doubt or a timid attitude. This program gets results!

You want to give back to your family and reward yourself with a better life. It comes down to **mindset** and **this training**. We're in the game to win.

You don't even need a Plan B, stick to Plan A. Through perseverance and dedication, you can reap the rewards that come from the How To Get Rich In Today's Real Estate Market course.

If you cling to another plan, or have reservations about your commitment to this program, then you think there is a safety net. This defeatist mindset will only weaken your focus, passion, and drive.

You don't need a safety net which will distract you. You must stick to the program to the gratifying end! That is where true success is created. You can never be successful until you start to focus in on one platform in order to make money.

So many investors fail because they don't know how to put blinders on. They get so distracted by numerous petty projects or with the idea that the next greatest, magical investing is going to make them rich.

You wouldn't go out and open five companies at the same time would you? No person has the capacity to achieve that level of commitment, concentration or work. The same analogy is true with your real estate business.

As we move forward, I want to encourage you to start looking at your goals and objectives. Ask yourself, "What is my plan of action?"

It is very important that you know what your end purpose looks like, what is it that you want to achieve, and how to achieve it.

Are you interested in supplementing your income with $40,000 or $50,000 a year? Are you interested in making $100,000 a year? Whatever those goals are, you need to put them in writing. Then work backwards so that you can reach that goal.

If I want to make $100,000 a year, I need to roughly bring in about $2,000 a week. To bring in an estimated $2,000 a week, I need to wholesale two lower-end properties, or one good-sized property in a decent neighborhood, per month.

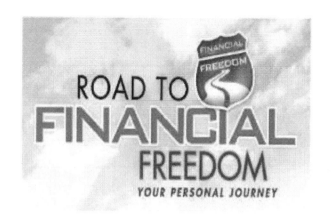

Continuing this line of thinking, to achieve one deal a month, I need to be making between 200 and 400 lowball offers a month. Also, I need to be doing marketing campaigns and driving around 100 qualified leads into my office every single month.

Get the big picture then look at the smaller details in reverse order. Your objectives need to be very clear and they need to outline what you want to achieve over the next six months.

There is also your daily plan of action. What is it that you are going to change in your day-to-day life right now that will free up your time and resources to allow you to focus on this amazing business model?

Listen, if you're not focused, there will be times when you spread yourself too thin. You may feel as if you are burning the candle at both ends. What can be removed, temporarily, out of your current life? Eliminate what is of lesser importance so that you can spend the time and energy with this new winning business plan.

Those are the three things I want you to take into consideration before we even get started. If you put in the required work, you will attain the goal of financial freedom. Furthermore, you will be able to reach back and help more people along this path of knowledge and independence.

Think about the thing you want out of life and start putting them down now! Let's work on this small exercise to get a better idea of the goals, income, trips, family time, personal goals you want out of life.

Goals	
Income	
Trips	
Family	
Personal	

Chapter 1: Why
Real Estate

Easy Way to Riches

Real estate has been one of the fastest ways to get wealthy in any industry to date. The ability to acquire properties at a discount is significant to this wealth building phenomenon, especially in today"s market.

This allows investors to obtain discounted properties significantly below market value and create a quick-turn profit between $10,000 to $50,000, with occasional revenue as high as $100,000 per deal!

 What you can earn with the ability to flip one piece of real estate can equal, or exceed, the average yearly salary of most of the population. This type of successful transaction allows you to jumpstart your financial freedom and put your family in a position for

Keep in mind that utilizing one of our four profit centers will stream-line your efforts.

In regards to a profit center of quick-turning or wholesaling, merely knowing the strategy of finding discounted houses and putting them in the hands of a buyer, who is eager to acquire that property for cash flow or remodeling, is the essential step.

This allows you, as a new investor looking to jumpstart you're investing business, to get out there and create an immediate profit.

I also want you to understand that this is a once-in-a-lifetime adventure for you. A venture that can be the most profitable endeavor you have ever taken in your life. This is an especially great time for success due to the current climate in today's real estate market. We will probably never again see such profit potential in our lifetime!

What do I mean by that? The real estate market has definitely taken a hit, but that only means that a shrewd investor is in a position to maximize on their investment.

With a fundamental understanding of the market you can really take advantage of some spectacular deals.

Properties are at such a discounted rate right now that they are producing tremendous cash flow and equity positions. People are gaining great riches right now.

Despite what you have previously heard or read about the real estate market, you need to understand that for most people who are trying to take advantage of creating wealth, there has never been a better time than the present to invest in real estate.

I want to be very clear, with the right direction, process, and guidance, along with coaching and mentoring, a tidy profit is possible.

> The fear that stops most people from getting involved in real estate is their ignorance of an easy-to follow, step-by-step process.

One of the many things I love about real estate investing is that it requires no formal education. It does not matter whether you have a doctorate's degree, a bachelor's degree, or no degree whatsoever; it is very easy to get started in real estate.

Real estate is a simple process of following a specific direction that will lead you to a path of success. These same processes will lead you down a path of achievement, and they will create amazing revenue for you.

Also consider this, real estate is the key to upward mobility because a successful, formula exists that works and has proven itself time and time again.

Numerous people have made millions of dollars following these processes, and you can too. I have students who easily make between $10,000 and $20,000 per transaction!

By following this training and putting my methods into practice, these associates have even made as much as $100,000 to $200,000! You too can follow in the footsteps of my prior students.

Any success formula is simply a process that has been proven over and over again. All you have to do is pursue the directions that I give you. Furthermore, if you implement these directions, you will start to see success in your life.

However, I want you to be clear about one thing; success does not come without implementation. It may be very easy for you to get off track. It may be very easy for your focus to get clouded.

You will see that by following these processes, your phone will start to ring with business proposition; marketing campaigns will start to work, and deals will come together.

Chapter 2:

Why Now Is the Time?

Why is now the time for investing? Because there has never been a better time! The secret to any successful niche is knowledge, knowing when to get in and when to get out.

This is the time to get in the real estate market. To be successful in real estate, you must understand the four profit centers.

Historically, we know how to determine the future by looking in the past. Applied to real estate, these are called market cycles and they are our best focal point to determine what is going to happen.

Previously, real estate has gone down and come back up with regularity. Right now, we are at the bottom of another market cycle. As before, the market will rebound. If you can get industrious and get into this market now, you can build immediate wealth with real estate investing.

Real estate is continually evolving over time. There are many new and successful methods, known as "new rich" to real estate investing while some of the old techniques no longer work.

I want to guide you down the path of becoming a "new rich" investor and really look at things from a broader point of view so that you can see the benefit of being in this real estate market

History will repeat itself; the market will sore to new heights. We are already seeing the first glimmer of the market upturn.

We did experience a tremendous collapse in real estate, but wise investors are noticing the market is on the way back up.

It is absolutely crucial to get into this market right now because real estate is going to skyrocket soon and produce more millionaires than ever

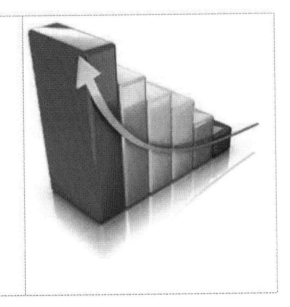

I am personally acquiring as many properties as I can manage right now because I know that this market will turn. When that occurs, I will be sitting on a huge goldmine above and beyond all my current assets.

You should be looking at this market as a challenge. Instead of a crisis, you should see a goldmine.

Take a lesson from the California gold rush. Everyone knew there was gold in the hills, but no one knew about mining. However thousands of amateur prospectors went anyways.

They learned through hands-on experience. They surrounded themselves with like-minded people and didn't give up on their dream. They went to the mountains and dug for gold, many hitting it big.

Overload of inventory

The foreclosure market is saturated. There is an all-time high of empty homes that banks need to unload. We can start acquiring properties immediately because our inventory is huge.

Banks have put those foreclosed homes back on the market. We are seeing a flood of properties coming our way.

Just the other day, I acquired a foreclosure property right around the corner from my house. It is worth about $300,000, yet I was able to purchase the property for $100,000.

Additionally, I put another $40,000 into it but I anticipate making a profit of $120,000 on this one transaction!

Now, what would $120,000 do for you?

 I highly encourage you to really take a good look at this market and understand that you can get extremely wealthy by just stepping into the real estate niche and start to acquire as many deals as possible.

Notice I didn't say "properties," I said "deals" because you may not be in a position to buy and hold properties.

You may not be in a position to buy a house and rehab it, but you can be in a position to find and acquire moneymaking deals, often with no money or credit needed.

There are many famous people constantly talking about how and why they got wealthy. They will tell you that you have to find a niche. You have to get in that niche, and you have to really stay ahead of the curve.

One of the greatest gentlemen in the world that understands niches better than anybody is Warren Buffet.

 Warren Buffet has always been able to find companies that are about to blossom. Mr. Buffet then buys shares and makes millions. He has been able to understand market cycles and what is and is not profitable.

Warren Buffet says, "When everyone is fearful, you need to be greedy; when everyone is greedy, you need to be fearful."

Take a look at this market, people are fearful; they are not doing anything. If you will go against the grain, you too will start to see what Warren Buffet sees while most people are paralyzed by anxiety.

Fear is really nothing more than false evidence appearing real. To overcome fear, you must educate yourself. The more you educate yourself, the less fear you experience as you move forward.

Chapter 3:

Taking Control of Your Life

Although you may be eager to jump into real estate investing and reap the benefits, I really want to make sure you understand if you don't have the right mindset, achievement of your goals will be twice as difficult.

Let's use a weight-loss analogy. If you knew jogging, weight training, and a regimented diet were necessary to attain your weight goal, but you lacked the correct mentally for the work and sacrifice, then you're not going to have long-term success.

There is a necessary responsibility and ownership if the sacrifice is to be a success. You have to continually focus on the ultimate goal.

Getting this sort of mindset in place is the number one priority! You have to really visualize that you can be wealthy, and above that, you have the right to be wealthy. Do not accept the view of doubters. You have to choose to be wealthy.

It's all about choices. We have the ability to choose anything we want out of life; we control our destiny with our decisions. We choose everything, from minor details to the grand plans.

Some who are not financially secure even choose which bill to pay each month. Those choices really control our destiny and influence the benefit or penalties we receive from those decisions.

For the real estate investor, choice is by far the most valuable tool we have at our disposal. You must choose right now to be wealthy with the real estate blueprint I will demonstrate.

You must choose to implement the things I teach you. You must choose to go out and become a real estate investor before you start to see the profits and influence you can exert in your life.

If you are looking for a new adventure, if you seek the greatest tool for generating wealthy, you have to choose to take the action.

 At the end of the day, most people are so bombarded with the daily monotony of life that they never get off the couch to make a positive change. We are still in the rat race of our job and everything else going on around us. We get overwhelmed.

You have to choose to remove something form your life. This new business model of real estate investing requires some time and effort. It will require some patience. Just like school, you must dedicate energy to making this business grow.

This is not a hobby; this is a business course with great potential profits at stake. When I say, "It is your choice," you must know that I mean "your choice to be dedicated and succeed'

Also, I highly recommend removing negativity factors from your life. When you are getting started in this business, some well-meaning people are going to share their opinion. They may think you can't do it or that the market is too risky.

These people don't know what I am going to teach you. Also, these are the types of people who never chose to be responsible to make a positive life change to benefit their families or the community.

We are constantly surrounded by negative people, sometimes friends sometimes family. This life decision is really about us and this negativity can affect who we become. Pessimism is like an infectious disease. We can catch it if we go too near the source!

As you move into a new adventure, realize that some people are not going encourage you to succeed. Often this is done with a twisted form of protectionism; they don't want you to be harmed.

Sometimes, however, this pessimism is due to feelings of jealousy or fear that your new life will lead to separation from them.

These people do not understand how you can step out of your current circumstances and into a whole new life.

When I was beginning my own investor's journey, I remember how quickly people became negative. Even before I tried this method other people said, "What is he about to do? Well, I'm not doing that, so he shouldn't do that." Fortunately, I did not listen to their doubting advice.

You need to make the choice regarding who you allow into your sphere of influence. Keep the doubters at arm's length.

A major key to growing successfully in any business or personal goal regards the people you surround yourself with. Encircle yourself with successful people who know how to raise you up.

Do you desire a higher financial lifestyle? How are you going to learn that from your poor acquaintances or family members? If you want to be successful, gather around successful people and do what they do.

Let's be frank, some people suck the energy and creativity out of your life. They suck time away from you keeping you from being a positive force and impacting other people.

You need to slowly remove yourself from these people's orbit. You don't need to be abrupt or rude, just manage your time and company in a manner that will bring you closer to the winners!

Personally, I have made it very clear who I allow in and who I don"t allow into my life. Some people only drain me. They slow me down and sap my focus and dreams to achieving the success I want.

I realize some of these negative influences may come from family.

However, if you really want to help the people in your life, then you need to help yourself first. There is no greater gift in the world that when you can help yourself financially.

Then you can step out and help other people, including family. You can start to direct them in a positive light and a more welcoming manner to show them how you achieved your success.

Success breeds success. Only then will they follow the path that you have created for them. It all starts with taking control of your life.

Chapter 4: Anyone

Can Do This

As I set out, exploring real estate as a wealth-building tool, I wasn't sure if I could do it. I really didn't know if it was possible for me to achieve the success that other people were telling me about.

However, I resolved to give it my all and overcome my early circumstances. I was hungry for success.

I grew up with a single mother who was struggling to raise two boys in a little town in Alabama. If I was to accept the standards of my community and be influenced by those I was surrounded by, then I should have grown up working on a farm (no offense to farmers), but that was not the life I envisioned.

Life is really what we make of it!

The destiny we choose to pursue will be the condition we achieve. I had higher aspirations so I set out to educate myself in real estate. I started looking at all the different ways to make money with the buying and selling of property.

Though I read many books on real estate, my greatest lessons came from practicing the hands-on approach I had studied.

From the get-go, I wasn't the typical real estate investor. I didn't even have a background in real estate. As I set out on my adventure in real estate, I was dead broke and had really bad credit. I needed the tools that required no money, to allow me to be a real estate investor.

The opening for me was wholesaling. Wholesaling is a unique strategy which allowed me to start generating immediate income with my business.

I began making five-, ten-, twenty-, even thirty thousand dollars per deal. Within six months of getting involved in real estate, I was able to walk away from my job.

Before things broke wide open for me, I was looking at a huge mountain of debt in front of me. However, I didn't focus on that mountain. I looked to the green valley on the other side of the debt mountain. I imagined that valley having waterfalls, fresh fruit, and warm weather year round.

This was the beautiful lifestyle I imagined I could live if I could just get over the debt mountain.

Along my journey, I kept educating myself. I kept finding new ways to get involved in real estate, and new methods to invest in properties without any money down or without any credit whatsoever.

These same, tremendous training tools are available for you to pick up and put into practice today.

Over time, my real estate business exploded. I was doing four to five single transactions every single month; even more some months. I was earning five figures a month without ever closing on a single house.

This allowed me to start building a new mountain, a mountain of cash which in turn generated new investments to accumulate even greater wealth. I would start buying cash-flow real estate and acquiring other companies.

It was an amazing transformation that a guy from Alabama, with no money and poor credit, could now own real estate all across the United States. I had five figures of cash coming into my bank every single month, even if I didn't get out of bed. I owe all of that to the education I acquired regarding the real estate markets and some unique strategies.

It doesn't matter where you came from, it doesn't matter who you are, and it doesn't matter if you have money or not. It doesn't even matter if you have bad credit. You can also do this business like these people who have followed my training. They are all successful real estate investors who started out just like you.

The first investor I'd like to introduce is Trish from Washington. I remember she was just trying to figure out how get into what we call the "new rich', this new age of real estate investing.

Trish was in the mortgage industry and realized the people she was getting loans for were making a lot more money than she was. She wanted to know more about what they were doing. Trish started wholesaling real estate. She followed what I told her to the letter and she started achieving wealth!

Zack and his team—I can't express how thrilled we are to have been introduced to Zack Childress. We have been dabbling in the real estate field for quite some time now, but needed to upgrade to the 21st century.

With Zack's wisdom, guidance, and true sincerity of wanting to help people succeed, we did and still do. In our backyard, we are now buying single-family residences and triplexes for literally pennies on the dollar thanks to you, Zack. I can't tell you how thankful I am for the guidance, the education, and the training that you have given me.

I just want to let you know on our very first deal after following your directions; I put $40,000 in my bank account. I thought that was amazing, but then I kept following your direction, and in the second deal we did; I put $165,000 in my bank. Zack, I can't tell you how you've changed my life just simply following the direction and the guidance that you have given me. Again, thanks for everything. It is a great life. It is becoming even better every day.

~Trish W., Washington

Stories like this are the reason that I teach people how to do this business. Being able to help someone put $200,000 into their bank account has dramatically impacted my life.

I want to introduce you to another gentleman named Abe. As a young, IT support person for a bank, Abe knew very little about real estate. When I first started working with Abe, he absolutely blew me away with the speed of applying his newfound knowledge. He was learning and retaining so much, it allowed him to put the program into practice.

Abe had never done a real estate transaction and wasn't formally educated in real estate. However, after a short learning period, Abe made his very first deal. I will never forget the excitement that he shared with us.

My name is Abe, and <u>after three</u> months of using Zack's easy-to-follow educational training, I am now wholesaling properties, and the checks keep coming in! I currently have _22 properties under contract, and I am looking to have several more closes in the next couple of months.

With Zack's education and training, the process was very simple to follow. I had a full-time job, and I couldn't have done all of this without his education on how to automate the process.

I was a bit intimidated to jump into negotiating, contracting, and selling properties, but rest assured that with Zack's training, it was all laid out for me. Money is no longer an object in my everyday life, and I owe all of that to Zack.

~Abe A., San Pablo, California

Now, that's a great story. It just goes to show, whether you have specific real estate experience or not, you too can successfully put this program into practice. This is exactly what can be done if you follow the training, and you use the tools that will be given you.

I'd like to actually give you another testimonial, this one is by Eugene. When I met this very intelligent man, he was working for a software company, traveling the world, negotiating contracts for a well-known company.

Eugene said to me, "Zack, I want to be in real estate. I want to invest because I want to be able to get away from the traveling and be at home with my family more."

I told Eugene, he had to find his why. Your why is the key to your success. It is what will drive you to be all you can be in this business. It is what will allow you to be in that mindset that we have talked about. I worked with Eugene as he followed the trainings and the processes.

> **My first deal: $20,000! Zack, I can't thank you enough for your support in pushing me to do more every single day. The training that you provide is by far the easiest process to follow. Your processes helped me be a better investor.**
>
> **With your help, I was able to do my first deal and make over $20,000 on it. I just want you to know that we didn't stop there. We continue to follow your training and put the processes in place that you teach.**
>
> **Simply by doing that, I now have another deal that will bring in even more than my first deal. I can't wait to see this year unfold and all the success that it will bring because I simply picked up a book and did what you told me to do. I can't thank you and your team enough, Zack.**
>
> **Eugene S., New Jersey**

Eugene's testimony is yet another great success story.

Guys, the reason I share these stories with you is because I want you to understand that by simply getting out there and doing something, success will come. Success will follow implementation of this program. This is what will separate you from all the other people.

You can't make a difference in your life without doing the actions first. Consider this carefully because it is very important that you understand, no matter what walk of life you came from. You too can do this!

Stay focused! Set a game plan and commit yourself to it 100%. Maximize what this book has to offer because, I want you to be more focused than a red laser light. That is really the key here.

Guys, it's time to move on. The next chapter is a great one because we're going to talk about the four profit centers of real estate. This is really where it all unfolds.

You will see the different tiers that are employed in being a successful real estate investor. Good luck, and remember, the secret is to implement what I teach.

Chapter 5:

Four Profit Centers in Real Estate

As you move closer to your goals as a real estate investor, there are certain things you must keep in mind;

1. How you look at every deal?

2. What is the exit strategy with which you need to be familiar?

This is the beginning of what we call The **Four Profit Centers**.

First off, what are these four profit centers and how can you utilize them for profit? They are:

Wholesaling/Quick Cash

Lease Option/Cash Now and Later   Rehabbing/Large Checks

Buy and Hold/Wealth Building Each of the four profit centers have their own unique strategies, too. Each has a different angle, which can maneuver into a variety of options and deals. Each has its distinctive different purpose and outcome.

1. Wholesaling

Wholesaling is by far one of the most desirable and easiest models because with no money or credit, you can create quick cash immediately. I still use wholesaling to this day due to the quick success aspect.

My wholesaling business is like an engine that I leave running. With it, I'm able to generate $5,000, $10,000, or even $30,000 extra per month!

I can then take that money and fund my other business interests or fund the wealth-building side of my personal life. My ultimate goal is early retirement, and the wealth developing aspect of wholesaling leads me closer to that dream each month.

Wholesaling is the functioning between two contracts: a Purchase and Sales Agreement, and an Assignment of Contract. That is all you need in order to go out and start creating cash right now! Your financial reward comes down to the simple concept of real estate investing.

2. Lease Option

Lease Options are what I call a "cash now and cash later" program. Lease Options are one of the most unique and creative approaches to real estate that I've ever found!

As with wholesaling, you don't need any credit with a Lease Option. You don't even need an income! There is a small amount of money required for many deposits, but that is a small inconvenience to pay for acquiring Lease Option property.

The beautiful part about lease option properties is that they are often not discounted like an actual true wholesale deal. The property simply needs to keep between 5-10% of it's equity in order for you to retain the property as part of a long-term lease.

Eventually, you will locate a "tenant buyer" who will close on the property at a later date. If you are managing a "Sandwich Lease Option," you will be paid up front as part of an "Option Consideration Fee." Furthermore, the payments will continue during the duration of the "tenant buyers" stay.

First, negotiate the tenant's monthly payment plan. You are free to be flexible with the tenant and meet their needs while earning a monthly profit for yourself. You want to research the average rental market in the area and add 15%.

If the 15% is greater than the agreed upon monthly payment, you should stipulate a down payment during the transaction process.

Another advantage of this lease option is that a final payment waits at the end of the tenant buyer's term of residence.

At the end of the transaction period, you are in position to allow the tenant buyer to close the sale and become the sole proprietor. The difference between your purchase price and the tenant buyer's negotiated price is your profit.

Not only is this very lucrative businesses relatively easy to become involved in, but you are helping people purchase a nice home of their own. Everyone comes out ahead; the seller, the first-time homebuyers, and of course, yourself.

Lease Option can also be combined with a wholesaling strategy to create a very unique niche. If your aim is to put the property under a lease option or under a Seller Financing Agreement, simply find the tenant buyer and assign them the rights to the lease or Seller Financing. They pay you a small fee up front.

You don't get paid nearly as much as with a Sandwich Lease Option, but you do get paid between $2,000 and $4,000 on the transaction allowing them to take over the property.

With wholesaling a lease option, you're not involved in the transaction beyond the initial transaction. You are not playing the part of a property management;

you don't have to deal with the headaches of repairs or the occasional troublesome tenant.

This blending of Lease Option and Wholesaling is something that many of our students have applied in markets that are high-end; markets like California, New York, Florida, or Arizona.

In these markets, houses aren't necessarily going to be great wholesale deals; being generally of higher value than elsewhere in the country, however, you can still acquire properties in these lucrative markets.

Just remember, a lease option deal is only going to work if the seller is feeling what we call a "payment pain." That means, they're not able to pay the mortgage and they need someone to take over the payment.

3. Rehabbing

Rehabbing is by far one of the greatest ways to quickly reach elevated success as a real estate investor. However, I must caution you, there are certain key skills and a thorough familiarity of this model that are crucial for high achievement in this niche. Also, you will need a power team in place to be truly successful as a rehabber.

Additionally, rehabbing can often go over budget. In fact, from my own experience, it never goes under budget. However, you're going to have a little bit more risk involved in rehabbing than you would just wholesaling or lease optioning. I can tell you this, though: the reward is much greater

If you are determined that rehabbing is your niche, you may want to find an expert in the field and partner with him at the start.

Say you buy a house for $40,000. Now let's suppose the market average is $80,000 and $100,000 on the higher end home. You can take that $40,000 house, remodel it so that it meets the standards of a higher end house. You can even add an extra bedroom or bathroom, pushing the value even higher. This is known as "forced appreciation."

You stand to make a tidy profit when you sell your $40,000 home for $100,000! Even minus the cost of the rehab, called a "hedge factor," of about 10-15%, you will earn a large sum for your efforts.

Furthermore, you can decrease that hedge factor to around 5% once you've acquired some experience and you've attained a basic knowledge of rehabbing.

Rehabbing is what investors call a Tier 3 model. You must have the experience and knowledge to successfully conclude Tier 3 transactions. There are potential risks but the rewards are great!

Initially, I suggest sticking to Tier 1 wholesaling. After a bit of experience and success, you can move to Tier 2. Before tackling Tier 3, it's important that you are comfortable and familiar with all the mechanics and elements.

4. Buy and Hold

Buy and Hold is the ultimate wealth-building model and it takes all of the other three profit centers to accomplish this Tier 4 investment.

At Tier 4 investor, you are now using the income and the resources from your other profit centers to acquire properties that produce cash flow.

You can start to generate a healthy passive income that, over time, will allow you to walk away from your job or retire early without financial fears. In fact, your steady passive income will be so great, that you will achieve your dream life.

The four profit centers make it possible for you to have a roadmap as you learn about marketing for sellers, finding investments, picking the right markets and researching properties, making offers, finding buyers, and closing deals.

Chapter 6:

No Money or Credit Needed

Getting Started Right Now

The key to this whole business model in general and the profit center in particular, is to really understand that you need to find the quickest way into your market. You need to start right now!

If that means that you're in a position to start buying and holding, I highly encourage that you do that. If you're like I was when I was getting started, no disposable income and little credit, then you really want to dive into the wholesaling model.

I love wholesaling so much because there is very little risk involved. When speaking of real estate, a lot of people say, "Well, risk is in real estate." That's true if you're buying and holding, or if you're buying and fixing to flip, or if you're going to redevelop some land. Each has a level of risk involved.

Wholesaling is the fastest, low risk way into the market. You can literally get started right away, without any of the standard risk formulas. All you're doing is selling your contract to buy!

All the traditional real estate methods require you to actually close on the property. But with wholesaling, you never close on the property.

The truest form of wholesaling involves dealing with a "for-sale-by-owner."

This is anyone trying to sell their house without an agent or brokerage house. Typically, this transaction property can be acquired at a discount.

Once the discounted property is obtained, you can find an end buyer, someone interested in acquiring the house as long term dwelling. You will be able to transfer your good deal into the hands of a great buyer, while picking up the spread in the middle.

This allows you to start creating cash right now. Wholesaling is the fastest way into the market. It takes very little effort for you to make this portion of your real estate investing dreams a fact.

One key component to keep in mind is marketing. You need to comb the market for discounted properties so you can acquire them. Some of the greatest ways to find these deals are:

☐ direct mail
☐ online leads
☐ run ads in the paper
☐ bandit signs

You can test all these types of marketing while looking for discounted properties. There are tons of diamonds out there, hidden in neighborhoods. They could be your neighbor, your family, or friends; they could be anyone who is in danger of losing their house.

There are going to be niche areas, like probate and expired listings for you to choose from as well. These avenues allow you to find really great deals as a wholesaler. Keep in mind that you are a wholesaler and acquiring properties at a discount. You are wholesaling them to landlords, investors, and rehabbers.

Your landlord list is going to be your best friend as a wholesaler for two reasons:

1) Landlords are the biggest buyers in today's market because they understand buy-and-hold. They understand cash flow, the markets and how they move, and they're prepared to hold a property until the market turns around.

2) Landlords are also great motivated sellers. A lot of people who get into buying houses as landlords get frustrated and overwhelmed. Sometimes they can't handle the process or they can't keep a tenant in the home. That causes them headache, therefore, they are willing to walk away from the property.

Those two factors are primary reasons why we go after landlords. They are a huge, lucrative market. I just want to point out that there are many different ways to find these great deals.

One of the best things you can do when you're starting out is to drive through the neighborhood. I call it "driving for dollars."

> 1. Coming home from work, you drive a new route every day, looking over various properties.

> 2. Visit the city next to your community on your way out of town. Stay awhile and drive around.

What you're looking for is telltale signs like overgrown yards, mail that's piled up at the front of the house, boarded-up windows, or letters that have been posted to the front doors.

These are all signs that a house could be vacant or even abandoned. You may even do a Skip search on the property address to find out who the homeowner is and begin mailing them.

The Process of Wholesaling

Wholesaling really breaks down to taking control of a vacant or vulnerable property. You must make offers to the property holder. You will never be a great wholesaler until you understand that you have to start sending offers.

You can:

e-mail

fax

Send a Letter of intent (LOI). An LOI is an easy, non-binding form letter. You are not obligated to purchase anything; it simply advises the homeowner that you're interested in buying.

You can also use a standard purchase agreement which obviously gives you a little bit more control than an LOI. However, if you're just getting started, you probably want to use a letter of intent (LOI). Lastly, I suggest an LOI because these generate more offers without any risk on your end.

As you start marketing, finding some deals, and sending our letters and offers, you'll start to get some responses to those offers. You must analyze a deal quickly and give the homeowner a set of options on moving forward. Typically, our options fall within one of two methods:

1) All-cash offer at a discount, or

2) a terms offer, meaning that the mortgage stays in place and that we take over the monthly payment, to be paid off by us at a later date.

These two options typically generate the best results in any negotiating strategy, but the more options you give a homeowner, the more likely they're going to be won over.

In general, the chance for a successful conclusion of a deal is improved with a higher number of options available to the seller.

As you engage the homeowner, look at the home, and analyze the numbers, you can move towards a guarantee that you're going to put an offer on the property. If all the factors are favorable, don't hesitate, get the offer out there.

Once that offer has been accepted, you're a real estate investor. Now it"s time to play ball!

Now that we have an accepted offer from the seller, we are now in control of the deal.

> We control that piece of real estate until the close date or for the duration of the due diligence period.

> I would highly suggest that you want a 30-day due diligence period and a 30-day close period, especially if you're dealing with a for-sale-by-owner.

Also, you want to include in any agreement that the buyer has the right to extend the close of this contract by two weeks. That gives you is an additional two weeks to close the deal and find a buyer.

Once we have interested buyers, we can give them the details and show them the property. Once the purchaser is ready to acquire the property, we need a contract with the buyer.

This contract is simply an Assignment Agreement, a one-page document that literally releases your right to the property, on contract with the seller, giving the new buyer the rights to close the contract with the seller.

You are in a contract with seller "A" on property XYZ. Next, you're going to release your rights to that contract to the new buyer. What we get in this whole transaction is an assignment fee.

Inside that Assignment contract you outline this assignment fee and the conditions for payment. The seller pays you the assignment fee and all parties walk away happy with this win-win-win situation.

However, always keep in mind: you do not want to get greedy. Your buyer needs to make money. If you make $2,000 or $10,000 on a transaction, that should be a happy day for you. If you are not greedy, your buyers will come back again and again. Your reputation will precede you.

This is a repeat-buyer business because as you acquire more properties, you will find more buyers looking for those properties.

Chapter 7

Setting Up a Successful Business

As we move forward through these chapters of training, you'll see that the process is a step-by-step blueprint. If you follow that method, your business will begin to expand. It grows legs, so to speak.

Lead generation will flow naturally and you'll have the security of knowing that your business is firmly established with a solid foundation.

The next topic of our course deals with the foundation of your business. Nine times out of ten, at the outset of your venture, you are the foundation. Meaning: your credit and your income are what the success of your enterprise is resting on.

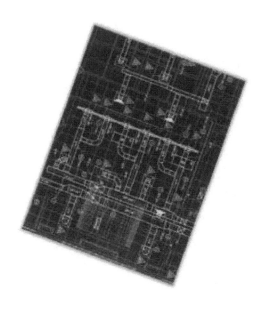

The survival of your business dream is going to depend on this during the initial phases as it grows and strengthens. Many times, the entrepreneur doesn't have money, or discretionary income, to get an enterprise off the ground.

In the budget building phase, it is vital that you discover the limit to which you can invest. How much are you able to devote to growing your business model. I promise, you will have to sacrifice something to move your business forward.

However, there are some constructive options for launching your business:

1. You must check your credit.

2. Establish professional contacts.

3. Set up your business structure.

4. Build a professional team around you.

Checking Your Credit

You want to establish a "three-score report." Many times, a mortgage broker can assist with this. Also, you can simply use some of the services available online.

You want to be sure that you are getting the credit report **plus** score. Each consumer is allowed access to one credit report per year. This will show you everything on your credit report. It is vital that you have this knowledge in hand!

You must really manage and monitor your credit. It is vital that you know what"s on that report and how it changes constantly. It is critically important that you establish and maintain a high credit score. This is the vehicle that will allow you to start buying and holding properties over time.

That is not the starting point but we need to work towards that end. We need to plan ahead. Establishing and building credit takes time. We want a great credit score in place down the road.

You need to:

1. Find out what your credit score is.

2. Determine if anything is false, misleading, or disputable.

3. If necessary, hire a company that restores credit scores. They will

remove unnecessary items from the credit report, thus rebuilding your credit.

4. Get quarterly reports of your credit score; stay appraised of what is going onto your credit report.

Follow these four points and you'll establish a great credit score that will only grow with your business.

Establishing a Professional Contact Network

In your business, you're going to determine what we call a "sphere of influence." This refers to associates and individuals beyond your power team, contacts and acquaintances with which you can do business.

Your power team is one crucial part of your business growth, but professional contacts, outside of your team are very important to your company's growth and success.

These are leaders or people of influence in real estate with whom you network and grow relationships. They are often other co-sellers, corporate or private investors. Networking is the key.

Join your local REIA clubs. Find other like-minded investors in your area and associate with that membership.

1. Find business groups in your area. Go to www.MeetUp.com and look for business, real estate, or related niche meetings in your local community.

2. Establish a positive influence within your professional spheres.

Determine what people are involved in, perhaps outings or civic activities and show up with the intention of meeting influential people. Charity events are a great community networking outlet.

3. Additionally, you want a social media campaign running. Get established on LinkedIn, Twitter, and Facebook! People you meet on these sites, especially LinkedIn, are highly professional contacts that you can niche.

These business contacts are going to grow with you. Furthermore, your contacts will bring additional contacts of their own. You sphere of influence will expand in ever increasing circles. You will be able to leverage the number of people you know in order to encounter even more people.

This viral network has become an essential business tool both physically, and on the Internet. A modern business will find it hard to thrive without a social media presence

As you follow this business model, your life will change. The petty things that once occupied your time and energy will no longer matter anymore. Your priorities will shift and change, thus moving in new and exciting directions in order to leverage your business capabilities.

Setting Up a Business Structure

From the beginning, understand what type of entity you want your business to be classified as. There are a variety of different structures to model you business on. Determine which is right for you. You may wish to seek out knowledgeable people who can help put these pieces in place.

Each structure is specialized, with certain strengths and abilities. As you learn the various configurations, you need to establish which is best suited for your business.

After some careful thought and planning, you will want to formally structure your business under one of these models. When it comes time to buy a house or flip a property, you don"t necessarily want to conduct the transaction in your own name.

Limited Partnerships

This is a partnership where one party has a limited liability, while the other is a sole partner. Limited partnerships are great for rehab projects. One invests the bulk of the money while the other performs most of the rehab work. Both want a partnership in the business but each has a specific responsibility or sphere of influence.

Limited Liability Partnerships

Very similar to Limited Partnerships, you"re working with partners who have less at personal stake and limited say-so in the business. They behave as a silent partner.

Limited Liability Company (LLC)

LLCs are the common form of business structure. The unique tool to utilize in this business model is asset protection. If you own real estate as an LLC, your piece of real estate is protected from outside lawsuits. Also, with an LLC, you can choose the taxable entity.

C Corporation

A C Corporation is established for small businesses that are quickly growing. The challenge is to determining whether this option is best suited for your purposes. You should seek a legal advisor to give you the best choice for your current situation. Unfortunately, a C Corporation is a very limited structure for the flipping of real estate.

S Corporation

Like the C Corporation, S Corporations are designed for small-based businesses and are very similar. However, S Corporations have some unique features regarding double taxation and tax entities. However, you must be knowledgeable concerning flow-through tax entity. Educate yourself thoroughly and seek business advice before choosing an S or C Corporation.

With each business structure, it's very important that you do seek a legal advisor in your area that can tell you exactly what you need to do for your taxable benefits.

Understand that as a real estate investor, when you're flipping houses, whether in your own name, as a corporation, or even as an LLC, for the purposes of the transaction, you have chosen your business to be an S or C Corporation for the benefits of flow-through tax entity. The profitable gained will flow through the entity straight to your income tax.

This could be detrimental to your investing business's growth if not handled correctly. You could possibly be labeled as a real estate dealer. There are several undesirable effects that come from being labeled as a real estate dealer:

Not being able to do 1031 exchanges.

Your taxable rate goes up, possibly as high as 40%.

You lose other benefits such as write-offs and concerns.

Be cautious when picking the corporate model entity. Make sure that if you aim to flip houses, your corporation mode will allow you to do so without the penalties of choosing a flow-through entity.

Building a Professional Team

Let's talk about building a professional team and the importance of having expert advice readily available. This is what I call a "power team." The power team is really a key network tool that is invaluable as you first getting started.

As you succeed in real estate investing, you will attract a larger, superior power team. If some people are not able to keep up with your business, you will need to replace them.

Some team members may be beneficial when you are just starting out but are not capable of sustaining the greater amounts of business that you are aspiring to.

Fortunately, your success will bring more experienced team members into your orbit. This is a good indication that you are doing the right things and are moving forward.

The kind of people you need on your power team include:

> a CPA
> a title company
> a banker
> a real estate lawyer
> an appraiser
> a realtor
> a mortgage broker
> a contractor/handyman
> an insurance agent
> investors/buyers
> property locators
> private investors
> a mentor

A **CPA**, Certified Public Accountant, can often double as a bookkeeper. This job is very important as you grow. In the beginning, you might not have one working in your office, but you need to establish a relationship with one outside of your office.

One of the best things that you should do to find a good CPA is ask for referrals. Go to the real estate professionals, title companies, and mortgage brokers in your market and ask them who they would recommend. A referral-based CPA is always going to be better than one you cold call from the phone book.

Bankers are critically important in your business. The close relationship we develop with the banker will build our credit. If you have developed a good rapport with a local banker, doors of opportunity will swing open.

Some of the best banks in today"s market are local or community banks. Though having a small base of capital to draw from, they are not as regulated as the larger banking institutions.

The local and community banks have greater decision making freedom. Also, opposed to the big box banks, the smaller banks do not get hit as hard by fines, fees, and taxes, or by variations in the economy and market.

When establishing a relationship with a bank, ask them, "What types of venture or properties are you interested in loaning money on?" Review several propositions and select which ones are in your particular niche.

This is the beginning of a working relationship in which each party understands and respects the other.

A **real estate lawyer** is key to your business. Some states operate more along the lines of title companies, which are essentially a real estate attorney as far as the state is concerned. You will need to do a little research to determine which is the best arrangement depending upon the state you live in.

If a real estate attorney is the better option, then look for young, hungry real estate lawyers! You don"t want to waste your time with the guys on the big billboard signs or in the big newspaper ads.

Look for the small ones; these lawyers are working to make a name in the industry, they will impress you with their drive and tenacity.

Talk to your **title companies**, if they serve your community. Just as with the CPA, talk to other investors and find out whom they recommend. Go with the company which will give you their time and attention. If you plan on using a title company or escrow company, I highly recommend that you interview several.

Determine up front if they handle demand funds and allocate assignments. Make sure they play by the same guidelines you practice. Interview them thoroughly.

The difference between lawyer and title companies comes down to size, an individual as opposed to a company. However, both handle the same areas of responsibility.

When you search for a good **appraiser**, use resources that will point you towards accredited, or referral basis appraisers. By utilizing www.Appraiser.com, you can find some good resources for appraisers in our area. Another good source of information is www.ServiceMagic.com. These two options will greatly help in your search to find quality appraisers in your market.

Realtors are good to have on your team. A solid realtor knows your objective and what will best suit your needs. The best place to encounter these realtors at an REI club meeting.

You may also talk to the realtor managers in your area; ask your mortgage broker, or get referrals from other investors.

Following up on referrals greatly increases the chances of establishing a working relationship with a real top-notch realtor. Explain fully what they need to be doing for you!

In a sense, you are forming a partnership with them. They may direct you to some available properties that you can invest in. This should be a win-win, working relationship. If a realtor doesn't seem enthusiastic, move on to another.

A Mortgage Broker is somebody with experience in the investing field. This is what's going to give you the most success getting a loan through. Look for experienced mortgage brokers. You need someone that has investor loans available now. You don't need red-tape and excuses!

Go to www.NAMB.org to check on a mortgage broker or his company. Also, it's very important that you ask for referrals. Someone else in your market, niche, or center of influence is demonstrating successful real estate practices; ask them who their broker is.

A Contractor and a Handyman is very important as well. If you need to add an addition, rewire something, or run plumbing, you're going to need specialized, licensed contractors. At the same time, a handyman is a reliable, jack-of-all-trades who is great for minor repair jobs.

Remember, these are relationships that you're going to build over time. Also, always ask for referrals. Keep in mind, you might locate the invaluable power team members at:

www.ServiceMagic.com

www.MisterHandyman.com   www.HouseDoctors.com

Insurance Agents are critical because your properties must have the appropriate insurance. When using private investors, they will want the property insured in the event that anything unforeseen happens. That way, their investment is covered. To find investor-friendly agents, go to www.InsuranceAgent.com.

Title company, if available in your area, also fill this role. An example would be First American www.FirstAm.com. I've worked with First American Title Company for five or six years and they definitely know how to work with investors.

It is still a good idea to talk to insurance agents or title companies to determine what type of investor resources they have to offer.

Investors and Buyers. In today's market, you want to build your buyers list consistently. Whether this is a physical or virtual list, collect potential buyers from your own backyard or from out of state. The important thing is to create a substantial list of contacts which may become clients.

Property Locators, also known as "bird dogs," can help you find potential properties, even if they are officially on the market! A good property locator is a powerful tool and with insight, proper use, and persistence, your property locators can bring you a lot of business.

Private Investors are another vital component. Listen well and implement the things I teach you regarding private investors. These fundamental financial backers of your business are literally in your neighborhood waiting on you to approach them with great deals. By correctly tapping into their resources, your business will thrive.

A mentor is obviously someone that holds you accountable. They keep you on task and do not slack up on you if you are missing the mark. A good mentor will direct your steps and keep you on schedule. Your mentor will keep a solid growth plan in place. They can help you determine whether you have a deal worth pursuing.

All the Tools Needed for a Successful Business

As your business grows, the necessary tools needed for further achievement will increase. Fortunately, as you succeed, the means and programs at your disposal will multiply.

For instance, what type of equipment do you need? A computer, scanner, printer, and a fax machine are a must, especially an integrated "combo" package. A good set up costs more, but will be essential as your business grows.

You will periodically need to scan a document into your e-mail. You will also need to scan your signature. You will need to fax and make copies. Again, I suggest that you get a three-combo package for your office equipment.

Also, you're obviously going to need a laptop so that you can work outside your office. I cannot express how imperative it is to have the capability to enter or search data while you are visiting potential properties. Fortunately, a good laptop is inexpensively in today's market, generally between $300 and $700. You can even purchase on eBay for a better deal.

Another item that is indispensable is a phone. A good cell phone is one of your greatest tools in this industry.

These items are essential to begin your business, but obviously, you may require a private work area with a desk. From this desk, you can do business: take phone calls, complete necessary paperwork, and launch your deals.

In real estate investing, you must be mobile. To do so, you need a solid e-mailing system, perhaps a free Gmail account. Gmail is accessible anywhere in the world by computer or phone.

Furthermore, other e-mail accounts may be forwarded to your Gmail account or your POP 3. Having access to e-mail from anywhere at any time is crucial.

The iPhone is practically a mini computer in your hand. Researching and viewing properties is literally at my fingertips. I can turn on my Guerrilla and send offers or send messages to my VA back at the office. These are unique features of the iPhone.

Plus, iPhone has some really cool apps that go along with real estate investing.

You will also want to have some type of e-faxing set up. Check out www.MyFax.com or www.eFax.com. Incoming faxes will be sent to your phone right away. Sometimes, speed is money and you want to react quickly to offers or proposals.

Google Talk allows you to give out marketing phone numbers different than your cell phone or private number. In turn, messages will be forwarded to your phone. Google talk will transcribe voice mail into an email viewable from your phone.

These basic necessities and tools are beneficial for the entry level real estate investor. However, as you grow, your equipment and service needs will grow as well. Fortunately, you will be generating the capital to acquire and maintain greater tools and services.

Chapter 8: Diamond In

The Rough

As we begin to look at techniques for finding sellers, there are additional avenues, beyond the ordinary methods to consider. Other resources and tools exist to maximize your marketing campaigns.

Consider budgeting in a way that will allow several paid marketing campaigns. These will certainly draw potential sellers to your attention.

Although there are some free techniques that drive traffic, I want to focus on marketing campaigns that promote your business and generate leads. You can actually buy property leads online.

As you"re working on your budget, look into all the available marketing campaigns. You may want to allocate resources, such as time and money, as you examine which you may be eager to implement for your business.

Also, calculate how many leads you have the capacity to handle. Determine how many leads you want, then modify your budget to cover this new, but profitable, expense.

Another unique tool is the Free Lead Generator that is available for immediate implementation. It"s as simple as going online and turning this Free Lead Generator on!

The Free Lead Generator will pinpoint specific Web sites, Craigslist among others, with a list of keywords. Next, it will start pulling in the traffic from those Web sites.

Within this traffic are many potential buyers as well. You should use this unique tool right away because it will create more efficient time management while increasing the number of leads for your business.

Other Resources on the Web

News Voyager is a web-based system that allows you to find newspapers online. By doing so, you can find some great deals without the wasted time of purchasing all those papers.

Beyond News Voyager, look for other wholesaler sites online. See what types of deals they list. Keep searching, there may be other sites that Free Lead Generator overlooked.

Other highly recommended sites are Postlets and My Property Pad. Also:

☐ www.RealQuest.com

☐ www.RealtyTrac.com

☐ www.ReoSource.com

www.DataQuick.com

www.foreclosures.com

To get access to another great pre-lead system, go to www.PropertyLeadsNow.com. You can even use the same discount code I use: **Z2895C11**. Signing up using that discount code will give you a markdown on all leads that you are able pull from their marketing service.

I've been using this company for over five years and I believe this is the quickest way to establish a significant base of leads for a nice discount. Furthermore, these leads prove to be highly motivated clients.

Audio Postcards

Audio postcards are by far one of the most unique ways of delivering your message. The beautiful thing about an audio postcard is this that your message is automated,www.Realtor.com or www.ForSaleByOwner.com won't give your e-mail to the seller, but you can send them a audio postcard.

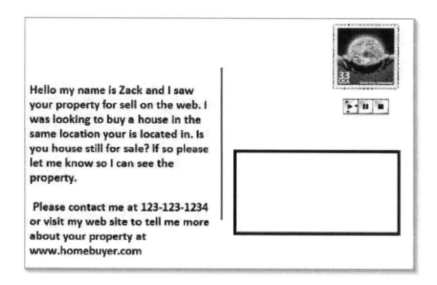

This audio postcard service is one more, eye-opening method of marketing yourself.

With your email, send an embedded audio postcard link for the reader to click on. It will play your message. Just remember to keep it short, simple, warm and direct.

That simple script, which you can record, has proven highly effective. Of course you can personalize it to suit your own style or the specifics of a unique deal. You may alter the message depending on whether you are contacting a potential seller, buyer, or realtor.

A great place to learn more about the reliable audio postcard system, is at this site: http://members.audiogenerator.com/specialinfo.asp?x=2110050

Bandit Signs

The power of a bandit sign: "I Buy Houses - Fast Offer Now." This can be a very lucrative business angle but it can be a very time-consuming creating and distributing bandit signs. However, the greatest challenge of a bandit sign really lies with the city ordinance:

1. Can you put up your sign in the first place?

2. Can you place small "hand-bill" or Yard signs? Can you use billboards?

3. Are you going to be fined for that sign?

Some investors have figured out the timeframes whereby they can put Bandit Signs up and take them down again over the course of a weekend so as not to be reported by city employees.

Putting a good bandit sign together requires some specific marketing concepts. The sign should not be over-crowded with information. It should be short, to the point, and eye catching.

Tell the reader what they need to do: a call to action. Of course, your web site should be prominently displayed and easy to identify and remember. For instance:

"We Buy Houses, www.CashOfferNow.com, 1-866-592-2429."

This ad does a very specific thing. It tells the reader what I do, it calls them to action, and it gives them ways to contact me. That is a simple but proven approach you can apply to your business model.

There is the expensive and inexpensive method of placing bandit signs. You can buy pre-printed yellow, corrugated plastic, or you can buy them by the hundreds in different sizes.

However, one of the most successful ways that I have discovered is to get plain white corrugated plastic, cut it down to a reasonable size, and handwrite on them with large Magic Markers. It's so simple it's brilliant!

I generally say something like "Need to buy a house" or "Must sell my house." It looks like a distressed homeowner or someone moving to the area looking to buy.

Hand-written messages appear more personable, you don't look like a big corporate company. Not only do you instill a measure of trust with the reader, but the city is likely to leave them longer if the sign looks to be from a private concern.

Tips for Putting Up Your Signs

1. Put your signs up in the exits and entrances to neighborhoods in your area. This is where people are going to be leaving from in the morning and coming back to in the evenings.

2. Located your bandit signs in the major areas in which you are looking to buy properties.

3. It's important that you post these signs in an area with heavy traffic exposure without placing them along a major road.

4. Track which signs and locations generate leads.

5. Implement this strategy immediately and often. **Newspapers**

Use newspaper classifieds and advertisements not only to motivated sellers or buyers, but to study market keywords as well. You should be looking at other wholesalers in your market; what wording do they use? Is their ad effective or confusing?

Simple phrases like, "We buy houses," or "I buy houses," are going to catch your eye as an investor looking for deals.

You may even contact the wholesaler directly to discuss joint venture options or cooperation. Build your relationships with other wholesalers immediately.

Direct Mail

Direct mail is one of the most powerful resources for hitting a targeted market of sellers, investors, and private investors. This can grow your business exponentially.

However, direct mail can be very expensive so I encourage you to use moderation. Don't accumulate a huge direct mail bill from the get go. As you reach early levels of success, modify your budget to include direct mailing.

You should start looking at direct mail as an additive to include in your marketing. As you implement these various forms of marketing, you are going to gain massive levels of marketing exposure.

Direct mail can result in a lot of wasted time and money if you're not handling it correctly. Create your direct mail campaign on a "stacked" and "linked" effect.

The stacked effect means that you are sending a piece of mail for your target market, say a foreclosure list, every week or at least every-other week. Follow this pattern over a consistent period of three to four cycles (three to eight weeks).

First, send a postcard. Next, send a letter. On the third mailing, send a second postcard with a second letter following that to round out your stack effect campaign. Although the pieces of correspondence vary, the recipients should mentally link them back to you.

Also, each should say at the top, "We sent you a postcard about a week ago, and we hope you received it. It's important that you understand that we can help you out of your situation."

Also, you should state, "In another week or so, we'll be sending you another postcard with some contact information. If you're not ready now, let us know when you receive the next postcard."

You're linking all this correspondence together in a way which communicates to the homeowner what's coming next.

You are reminding them of what has already been sent. They will begin to look for your correspondence. You are creating a relationship with each postcard and letter. The recipient begins to feel that you can be trust and perhaps, you can help them with their housing problem.

One of the most powerful postcards that you can use is simply a little yellow postcard with a straightforward hand written message in black ink.

The postcard should have a headline: "I can help. Do you need help? Are you losing your house? Quick! Call this number immediately. Foreclosure Prevention Company."

If you're targeting landlords, you may say something along the lines of: "Didn't collect your rent? Need help with rent?" This sort of message will catch their attention.

In the body, you want to be very specific about how you can help them and how your company is a stable and solid company.

At the end of the postcard, give them a call to action. Tell them what to do and give them a phone number and a web address to your landing page.

Believe it or not, people subconsciously like being directed to a specific action. A clear call to action produces good results. Just keep the action step simple, too many procedures and your person will lose interest.

Types of Direct Mail Marketing that You Should Be Doing Right Now

Let's look at some direct mail marketing niches. If you do not have a specific niche in which you are interested currently, I encourage you to try a variety of direct mail markets.

Just follow the direct mail procedures and get a list to start mailing. This might even point you towards a specific niche that you might like. Direct mailing could be very beneficial to the growth of your business.

Foreclosure List

A foreclosure list is very unique. Listings are divided into categories of 30-day, 90-day, and 120-day late, and late pending. Each variety will have specific variations to keep in mind when contacting the seller or bank. I suggest starting a 30-day or 90-day late list. These lists can be found at www.ListSource.com.

Free and Clear

Free and clear lists are also a great list with which to start your marketing campaign. Free and clear people own their property outright and often offer a great wholesale deal since they are not concerned with the paying of a bank note

Occasionally, this sort of property is in poor shape. If that is the case, you can create a partnership deal to rehab the property. Even after splitting the profits, after selling, you still stand to make a tidy income.

Expired Listings

Expired listings form a unique niche that is possibly your best list choice if you"re running a lease-option campaign. However, these lists are difficult to acquire and highly sought after by your competitors.

Have an agent pull an Expired List at www.TheRedX.com. Only agents have access to this resource, so you will probably end up paying some sort of commission or working in a partnership.

This isn't necessarily always the case, but some agents will want a form of compensation or portion of the profits in return for accessing the Expired Listing. If you want to rehab the property, you may even need a third team member, spreading the profits a little thin.

Non-Owner Occupied Properties

A non-owner occupied property list is simply a list of currently vacant houses. You can get these lists from www.ListSource.com. You're specifically looking for people who have owned the dwelling longer than three years. After a period of three years, the non-owner occupied property is a nuisance to the title holder; they are generally highly motivated sellers!

If you can find a non-owner occupied that has been vacant for seven years, the owner will have maximized any equity from the property. They will want to unload the property and move forward with their life. Again, check www.ListSource.com.

These are just a few lists but if you start utilizing them, you will start to see some highly-motivated sellers showing an interest. Such lists allow you to increase your marketing campaign and lead generation.

You should be receiving leads from a variety of different directions, but as I've stressed before, you must apply this invaluable technique!

Chapter 9:

Knowing When A Deal Is Profitable

Before you begin researching a property, you must determine the solution to that property. What is your goal with this acquisition? Are you looking to wholesale, resell, rehab, or buy and hold?

Once you determine your overall strategy, you will need to analyze the property, check the spread sheets, and run the numbers. In some cases, the property may not be worth your particular vision, in which case you can choose a different avenue or move on to the next property.

Finding the Solution

Looking at the solution to the problem is always going to determine your exit. If the house is a wholesale-based property, you"re always in a better position when you have multiple ways to exit.

Obviously, the homeowner will be pleased with the multiple options strategy in which he can unload his property. For example, if the homeowner has no equity but is in a position to hold the note, you will be in a position to run the numbers based on a Lease Option.

Using Spread Sheets

Since you're not directly connected to a title company or a title vault, you want to use several online resources when you're running information. These sites will help you determine what a property's real and potential value can be.

Some of those resources are the following:

- www.Zillow.com
- www.CyberHomes.com
- www.Eppraisal.com

With these services, you must be very clear that you're not basing hard numbers off the "estimator." Each of these services has a research box inside of the website that will have comparable sales data on sold properties.

This is where you determine what your property's value is going to be by comparing properties of like condition, location, and square footage; number of bedrooms and bath. This will give you remarkably accurate data by using these free information services.

It is imperative that you, as an investor, look at the cash flow on every property. This allows you to determine the position that you can offer the property to a landlord buyer.

For example, if you have a $100,000 value property but the seller can only sell it for $80,000, obviously, that is not a wholesale deal. However, if you can establish cash flow on that property, you still have a marketable property to a landlord in your area.

How do you determine if a cash flow is possible on a property?

1. If you buy at a price that you requested, what is the mortgage payment on the property? This will determine that you need to collect rents higher than your mortgage.

2. If you're able to attain a Lease Option, what is the payment going to be when you take over the note on that property?

www.FinestExpert.com

www.RentOMeter.com

These two services will allow you to acquire a property's information based on the rental market. You can then plug the property information into the website and receive the comparable rental market in that area. This will establish the "ball park" figure around which you can base the property's rental rate.

You must have accurate data on the property in order to better run the numbers. You will start to see your exact position with the property and what options are before you. Running accurate numbers can also determine the feasibility of continuing with your current plan.

For instance, perhaps the numbers indicate that a property would not be profitable as a rehab project but it may be a profitable wholesale home. Look to the numbers to increase your knowledge and strengthen your position.

When running your numbers, remember to run them based on different criteria.

1. First, run them based on a wholesale deal if it can be purchased at a wholesale price.

2. Second, run your numbers as a retail deal determining whether or not it can be sold at a retail price, and what your price point is when you purchased the house.

3. Third, run your numbers based on a Lease Option.

4. Fourth, run your numbers on a Buy and Rehab.

Run your numbers in different ways and know your exit. Keep your end goal in mind but don't let your particular vision cloud your thoughts. Look at what the numbers say. **Always** run your numbers.

Chapter 10:

Putting A Million Dollar Buyers List Together

As we move through the process of finding discounted real estate, motivated sellers, analyzing, negotiating, and making offers, as a new investor just getting started, you may be most interested in the wholesaling process.

The wholesale model is generally considered the best way to gain experience and knowledge before tackling the more complex modes of real estate investing.

The wholesaling process of real estate is really the beginning stages of any Creative real estate transaction.

You simply assign your rights to a contract to a new buyer who is willing to close the deal quickly. Those buyers may seem scarce at first, but if you are looking in the right places, the clients will surface.

There are plenty of buyers in the market today; all you need to do is reach out to the right places. There is a portion that may seem like potential buyers at first but prove to be a false lead. Don"t be discouraged if a promising lead evaporates, there are plenty of buyers in the market.

Those buying in today"s market are prepared for long term holds. Typically, those buyers are landlords or cash buyers, and there is a profitable market for dealing with them.

Landlords are buying in order to close on properties which they want to put into their portfolios and hold for a period of time. Landlords comprise, by far, one of the most lucrative buyers lists you can have on your database. They are not so much interested in discount property as in potential cash flow.

Cash buyers are purchasing homes in order to close quickly for rehabbing and resells.

There are a couple of ways we can find landlords and cash buyers.

One way to find landlords is to look for HUD opportunities. You can always go to the HUD website www.HUD.gov. This site list landlords in your area.

Many landlords are Section 8 buyers whom you want to reach. One way is to work with your local Section 8 office to find buyers who would be interested in buying your properties. Another way is to visit www.HUD.gov again and locate the listings for your city or county.

If you can find the Bid Results and Bid Statistics section, it will save you a ton of time. This information is between the list dates and closing dates. You must keep a database of each new listing so that you track it on sites like HUD.

Next, determine when that listing came off of HUD. The date of listing and date of home selling is our indicator that a landlord bought the property. Typically, about 60 days from this sell date, the home should start closing.

From this point, you will be able to determine who bought the house. You will know if the house was bought by a landlord. Then, you can track-back cycle on the address which will allow you search for the seller.

Working with landlords is another great tool when it comes to obtaining a larger list of landlords using the Internet. The site www.ListSource.com is one of my prime list-building methods for landlords.

This is an online list broker that allows you to log in and scroll down to Non Owner Occupied Properties. Typically, 90% of people who have acquired a loan as a Non Owner Occupied loan are those who have renters in that property.

Once you acquire a list of landlords, you need to sort this directory to better maximize the active landlords in your area. Once you are inside the Non Owner Occupied segment of List Source, you will have to fill in specific qualifications.

One of the things we are looking for are people who have purchased in the last 12 months. We want active investors who are buying properties in today's market. Also with this service, you can search for landlords by zip code, state, city, county, and postal code.

Once a date range is selected, you will be asked for a price range. Put in the typical price range of the area wherein you are marketing. If your median price range is $100,000, you will look for investors who have purchased houses between zero and approximately $150,000.

Other criteria to consider includes: what types of properties are selling? Typically, we want properties that produce cash flow; for instance, single family dwellings, duplexes, triplexes, quadplexes, and apartment buildings. All of these have a revenue stream produced by putting a tenant into that property.

You will also want the mailing and property address of the estate. With this list in hand, you can determine how many landlord buyers are in that market. Some potential buyers may not seemingly meet your standards or expectations but I suggest that you continue working off the largest list possible. You can purchase this list and then start mailing these landlords.

Another great way to focus on building your buyer"s list is by seeking out other wholesalers in your local market. You can share resources and leads. This may also lead to some joint venture enterprises. Co-wholesaling is, one of the fastest ways to get your business off the ground.

You will also want to search and join your local REA clubs to meet with fellow investors. You can establish strong relationships in this field that may become profitable at some future date.

While you are networking, you Should also communicate with your fellow real estate professionals and let them know what you are doing and how you want to grow your business. You will start to build a greater referral-based business where associates bring potential buyers to you.

Never underestimate the power of networking with professionals and even your family. There is literally a network of professionals all around you: doctors, lawyers, attorneys, dentists, and many others.

They all understand what investing can do for their future. It is your responsibility to make sure they recognize what you do and how you grow your business.

Let it be known that you are at their disposal if they wish to buy investment properties. Help them understand that process and how it can benefit them.

However, family may take a bit longer to convince, they will want to see a track record before determining your creditability. In time, they will acknowledge your success and do business with you.

No matter the source of your list: www.HUD.gov, landlords, or cash buyers, you need to be mailing them continuously in order to market your services and become a known quality.

Once you have acquired a list of buyers, mail them twice in the first month and once a month every month thereafter. When including a website, send them to a landing page that captures other pertinent information.

Chapter 11:

Closing A Deal For A Pay Day

As you make offers and deals start to materialize, you need to concentrate on getting the deal closed. All your marketing, networking, and analyzing will be of no use if you cannot close the deal. Everything will have been a waste of time.

Closing the real estate deal involves: preparation, planning, and outsourcing.

Preparation involves organizing a file along throughout the course of the deal. As you move through the transaction, you should construct a file on every property.

That file should consist of:

>Any faxes or copies of documents needed for the property.

>Copies of all contracts.

>A copy of any addendums.

>A copy of the assignment fees.

A copy of any deposited checks.

A copy of any appraisals or inspections.

You should also have a stapled copy of a check sheet, outlining the buyer's contact and pertinent information, contact e-mail and phone numbers, and seller contact information.

Also, include any co-wholesaler' contact information. Do not forget contact information for all agents, mortgage brokers, title companies, or attorneys involved. In short, anybody involved with the process

Lastly, enter the contract's effect date, the date of your contingencies or due diligence period, and the date of closing!

With a thorough, complete file, the brokers, title agents and attorneys will recognize your professional preparation and willingly work with you on future deals.

If you are working with a virtual assistant, scan all this information into a desktop file including the check sheet. Send the file to your virtual assistant who will be handling this transaction. To find a really great person to handle virtual transactions, I recommend:

www.TeamDoubleClick.com

As you prepare that file, it may feel like the deal is ready to close. Double-check to make sure you have all of the appropriate documents and contracts before the transaction moves to escrow.

Evaluate whether this deal requires any additional documentation: do you need to have a Demand of Funds on file because you will be paid out of escrow?

If so, make sure that the escrow company is working with Demand of Funds. In my course, you will have a Demand of Funds document. This can be filled out, signed, and delivered to the escrow company.

Also be aware of the conditions of the transactions. Other documents may be needed. For example, if the deal involves an A to B, B to C close, your title companies should be informed, and you need to have copies of all documentation.

Early in the transaction, ask questions of the buyer and seller, making sure you understand the specific timetable, costs, and additional fees and factors. Do not be caught unaware.

Make sure that in a transactional funding closing, the buyer has prepared to close the deal himself. Prepare the transactional funding with the title company and fund institution ahead of time. Do not wait until the last minute. Come into the closing calm, prepared, and professional.

Prepare your closing ahead of time, without the excitement and distraction of the imminent closing. Make sure you have all your "T's crossed and I's dotted."

Open escrow requires escrow money. Require a deposit from the new buyer equal to or greater than the typical escrow deposit of $500 or $1,000. When escrow opens, you are really using the new buyers' money.

If the transaction will be closed through a title company or an attorney, take a deposit or half of the assignment fee up front. Cash purchases will not require upfront fees for closing.

Upon opening escrow, I am continually asked, "How much money do I put into escrow?" You should put as little as possible into opening escrow. The less money tied up in escrow, the more profitable the final transaction.

Remember, escrow deposits are always negotiable! Agree on the escrow deposit with your buyer in advance and wait until the very last minute to open our escrow with a deposit.

Also, when opening escrow, make sure the escrow conditions are in the same terms as the agreement and contract. Feel free to communicate with your title company. You must be on the same page when the transaction goes to close. Minimize any miscommunication or confusion.

However, when dealing with an escrow officer, always be professional. Do not quarrel or needle unnecessarily.

Present all the required documentation in an organized folder. They will want to work with you again if you are prepared, organized, and professional. They will treat you as a professional real estate investor and a profitable working relationship may develop.

Another thing prepared is a Release of Funds. If the transaction does not close, you are still within the contingency period; if you decide not to move forward with that deal, request an Escrow Deposit Release or Escrow Closing Disclaimer.

Once you have a Release of Escrow Funds letter from the title company, fill it out and return to the title company. Being inside the contingency period, they will release the escrow funds.

One last unique niche to be aware of is Demand of Funds transaction. A Demand of Funds (DOF) letter allows a buyer to step in with the seller and get financed. However, you cannot assume that every title company will work with you on a Demand of Funds deal.

If the opportunity for a Demand of Funds transaction arises, be up front with the title company. Make sure they work with Demand of Funds, Assignment of Contracts, short sells, lease options, or whatever your specialty niche is.

Be forthright, do not assume anything. Better to be rejected early and find a new title company than to get to the closing period and have the deal fall through.

One last option is a virtual closing coordinator. This is what I call my silent partner. A Virtual Closing Coordinator is the person you will hand all of your transactions to. They work with your business to make sure that transaction gets closed.

They will follow up with all the people in the transaction: buyers, sellers, lenders, realtors, mortgage brokers, attorneys, and the title company. They make sure everyone is on the same page and all is moving forward in a positive manner.

Once you hand the transaction off to this "babysitter," you can begin focusing on the next deal. When your deal reaches the escrow, you can hand off the responsibility to your Virtual Closing Coordinator so that you can concentrate on growing your business.

Chapter 12:

Making $10,000 to $20,000 per Month Putting the System in Place

From your reading so far, you're probably extremely excited. However, don't let that feeling fade before you get out there to "play the game." First and foremost, however, you must have a plan. Also, you must dedicate yourself full-time in order to start generating $10,000 to $20,000 a month with real estate investing.

The most important part of the whole business model is the plan. You must be knowledgeable, focused, and prepared before acquiring properties and growing your new business model. This starts with a couple of key factors.

Marketing:

You need to do some marketing! Coming into your real estate investing business, you are an unknown element. People generally do not trust the unfamiliar.

The more people can see your name and identify it with a particular business or niche, the more trust and credibility you will build. In time, with proper marketing, you might even turn your business into a brand name!

Equipment:

From the outset, you will need a good phone and computer, both with Internet access. Furthermore, a scanner, printer combination is vital. Access to specialists, your power team, will also require capital.

Budgeting:

Without a budget, you will not be successful. Instead of generating this $10,000 to $20,000 per month, a business without a budget will most likely go under. For instance, if you spend $300 a month for advertising which produced 10 leads, one of which turned into a deal netting $5,000, logic follows that next month you should spend $600 on marketing in order to generate 20 leads.

At the end of each month, analyze your budget: what worked well, what areas should you reinvest resources, which areas should you increase or decrease the budget, and are some expenditures no longer worth funding?

Also understand that other things in life my need to be sacrificed in order to stick with the budget. Certain pleasurable, but non-essential, hobbies or trips may have to be cancelled in order to pump more money into the budget.

This is not wasted capital that you're spending here. This is an investment into your business and into your future. Once your business has grown to great heights, you can revisit all those pastimes you have sacrificed for long-term gain.

By reallocating money into your budget, you will create more wealth. "It takes money to make money."

Time Map:

From the onset, you must start with a time map, or time budget. Really map out your day, blocking time spots devoted to your business. You will begin to realize where you're wasting time throughout your day and how to maximize that time in order to accomplish your goals.

Each of us wastes so much time each week. It may not seem like much, an hour here, an hour there. After awhile, the missed opportunities and wasted effort of that time adds up.

Just imagine what could be accomplished by making use of each minute. Sitting down with calendar or organizer can maximize the potential of your day. You'll start to achieve more out of the week than you even thought was possible.

You must stay consistent with your marketing budget and time blocks! This reliability is what will actually create the wealth that you're looking for.

Consistently sending out offers, analyzing your deals, marketing, hanging bandit signs, doing newspaper ads, and driving for dollars, will pay off big when you're earning $10,000 to $20,000 per month.

Unfailingly sticking to the plan, your budget, and your time management is the key to success!

Making an offer:

If you do not make offers, you are not in this business, plain and simple! Also, the more offers you make, the more deals you will get, and the more money you will generate.

It may be a huge fear of yours to get out here and start sending offers, but how else are you going to achieve that $10,000 to $20,000 a month income without sending offers? If you never make an offer, you'll never get a deal.

The key: the more offers you make will be a direct reflection if how much income you're going to earn!

As you build this business model and market yourself, deals will come along. You can't sit and over-analyze them. You must start sending out offers.

Inside your contingency period you have a due diligence, and that will allow you to analyze that property. Offer first, conduct the deeper research and analysis second! The number-one mistake 90 percent of investors make is they never make offers.

In order to save time and energy, you can make your offers through a service. One of the best services I recommend, and use myself on a regular basis, is www.Co-Wholesaling.com/ADM .

As soon as you utilize this service, you will see that the entire offering process can be automated including the lead-generating process. The key to maximizing you're time is to automate and leverage as much of your business as possible.

Chapter 13:

Cashing in on Cash Flow

The ultimate goal you want to achieve with your real estate business is consistent cash flow. In your wealth-building model, real estate not only delivers cash flow on a monthly basis but it also delivers in the long-term with equity gained on the property and tax write-offs.

The faster steady cash flow is created, the faster you can leave your job. Obviously, the more wealth you possess, the easier your life becomes.

As you build this business, always come back to the things that produce cash flow. Your ultimate goal is wealth building.

Once you generate a little bit of cash flow through your wholesaling business model, take that cash and buy cash-flow producing properties. If you can purchase wholesale properties on our own, fantastic; if you partner with someone else, that's fine, too.

Just getting the first transaction under your belt is absolutely the greatest thing that you can do in business. Use that momentum and sense of victory to propel you on to the next deal.

Every business empire begins with the first success, no matter how small. From the start, focus on completing that first deal.

Think about it like this: if in your market, properties range between $20,000 and $60,000, you could typically produce easy cash flow on those properties. Even if this does not describe your particular market, there are other niches in which you can acquire a cash flow property.

If a house is $40,000, then you could easily acquire that property with $4,000 to $8,000 down. By wholesaling, you can generate the money needed to buy that cash flow property.

In the previous example, if you buy a $40,000 house and you put $8,000 down, your note will be $32,000, causing your mortgage payment to be around $250. You could probably rent that same property for between $400 and $500 a month.

Remember, this is a building process. If you could bring in $200 of cash flow from one property, imagine repeating this process through 10 properties. You would have a net cash flow income of $2,000 a month. Extend this model over a 24 months period. The lifestyle you want will be clearly within reach.

Wealth is the ultimate goal that people all try to reach. We all want to sit back and more fully enjoy our lives, spend time with our family and friends, and leave a legacy to our children.

You have to start your wealth building model with one property to generate cash flow and then move on to the next. In the long-run, you will build a successful business and create your wealth.

Moreover, real estate investing will enable you to retain that wealth. Look at your property profile and see which properties are producing cash flow on a consistent basis and which ones are not.

Eventually, get rid of the properties that aren't producing and replace them with a new portfolio of properties. Keep the good and replace the bad.

Another thing you need to consider is reinvesting in yourself and your business. As your real estate holdings start producing cash flow, you may find that your business has hit a plateau. At this point, you need to reinvest in your business:

Acquire a property management company.   Hire or contract with a property manager.

Develop your own management team and maintenance team to insure your properties are in top form, allowing the maximum amount of cash flow.

Your initial goal should be to equal your income. Approach it this way, you should be wholesaling enough properties per year to equal half of your income, and acquire enough cash flow real estate to equal the other half of your income. I call this a 50/50 split.

For example, if you're earning $50,000 a year, you should be producing $25,000 a year in wholesaling, while bringing in another $25,000 a year in cash flow properties.

That's going to average $2,000 a month in wholesaling and $2,000 a month in cash flow. Once you decide to leave the corporate job, you can start to grow your real estate business full-time.

Now imagine that half of your $2,000 a month comes from five properties equaling $200. The other half could come from seller financing deals that didn't require a loan. The key is to acquire as many cash flow properties as you can.

Compounding your business growth efforts and acquiring more real estate can easily be accomplished through additional means: seller financing, wrap-around mortgages, and lease options. There are at least 25 different ways that you can purchase real estate with no money and without acquiring a loan.

Next, bundle those up together, into what's called a 1031 Exchange into an apartment building. Starting with the purchase of a single property, and then acquire three, then five, ten, and finally, fifteen.

Now bundled them together and 1031-exchanged them into an apartment building. Immediately, all 15 of your units are under one roof, which is easier to manage, maintain, resell and increase rent.

However, don't stop with one apartment building. Repeat the process until you own numerous buildings. The procedure is proven and not overly difficult. Just duplicate the steps again and again.

This is truly the process of implementing and repeating a successful formula. As you effectively wholesale and generating leads and close more deals, your bottom line will grow dramatically. Pump that additional cash, into even more cash flow real estate.

At some point, you should look into the larger unit niche. You do not have to compete with the large investors going after 100+ units. The 10 to 50 unit buildings are a great market that is often overlooked.

See, many new investors really don't want to get involved beyond four-unit, or maybe eight-unit, apartment complexes. What's left in the middle is a whole untapped market of 10 to 50 units. That is a market that you want to move into as you build your cash flow model.

Building this sort of cash flow consists of:

Buying cash flow real estate

Buying cash flow real estate with cash or through a small loan for the deposit.

Lease options

Lease options can produce cash flow because you get paid through the spread, meaning you're paying the monthly mortgage payment compared to what you're acquiring on the back end as the new tenant buyer pays you.

Apartment buildings

Apartment buildings create an instant income for you through multiple units creating cash flow rents per unit.

Commercial space

You can go into any commercial space with what's called a Master Lease. A Master Lease allows you to rent the whole building at a discount. The tenants already in place are paying their normal rents, producing cash for you.

Land Rent

You can lease or option land and rent advertising space on that land, especially if it's along a major road or highway. You can even lease it out to people who want to use it for storage space.

Cash Cows

Cash cows are generally mobile home parks, storage units, Laundromats, and car wash facilities. These types of industries create huge amounts of cash flow through rents and fees charged for their use.

Don't feel that you must go and acquire all these properties right away. Begin with that first transaction!

Also, create a two- or three-year plan.

1. Year one: establish your business model, preferably a wholesaling business. With your first few transactions, start paying off some debt, increase marketing, and positioning your business to acquire more properties.

2. Year two: begin taking some income from the wholesaling business and start buying deals that will produce monthly cash flow. Perhaps conduct some retail sales, thus creating a greater amount of revenue. By the end of year two, start acquiring some significant cash flow in your business model.

3. By year three, you may be a tier-four investor. Your holdings should contain some true wealth-building properties. Now, you can actually start acquiring some other cash flow cash cows.

Chapter 14:

Taking It to the Next Level

Its game time and I want you to get off the bench. Run this business model, and make your business work. Educate yourself and implement what you learn. Market yourself, put things into place, build your power team, and find those diamonds in the rough.

Decide which one of the four profit centers will best fit your needs, but by all means, get out there!

If you keep doing the same things you've always done, you're always going to get the same results that you've always received.

The definition of insanity is constantly doing the something over and over and over again, expecting different results.

This however is a new world. You have the choice to change your destiny. Your destiny lies in front of you and it is at your fingertips. I encourage you to take as much power, time, and energy that you can find and put it into this business.

I can't even explain to you the lifestyle that comes with everything that I have been able to achieve simply by taking action and getting into real estate investing.

I want you to understand, too, that there has never been any successful person in life that didn't take action. The people who want to achieve new and greater things out of life are the ones that get off the couch and go do something.

They're the ones that put in extra time and sacrifice to make a change, getting up early and working late. However, by taking action and implementing the steps, you, too, will start to see results.

Nothing in life will ever come for free. There is definitely a price to pay. And you have to understand that you will have to give up something. Your life is the way it is for a reason. To change that path, you must sacrifice time, resources, or hobbies to bring this new real estate business into your life.

Keep in mind that this is a working process. At first, you will feel like an employee of your business. Still, you need to have the ability to step back and work on your business and not in your business.

The power of working on your business is the power of duplication, leverage, and growth.

When you're working in your business, it's impossible to see the big picture: what's working, what's not working, or how much time you're committing per project.

You need to understand how to start outsourcing and leveraging: using assistants, bringing in interns, and finding people who want to do the same things you do.

Surrounding yourself with those people will allow you to have that energy level and focus to really grow your business.

Don't get overwhelmed, each day is a new day. As long as you're working a bit every day, your business will progress. I used to think to myself, "How in the world am I going to build this business?"

I was focused on how much work was involved plus I still had an outside job. I reasoned that if I just got up earlier and did a little bit in the morning, and a little bit more at nights and on weekends, than over time this would start to turn into something.

It's like planting a seed: you have to nurture that seed, giving it a little water every day and planting it in good soil. Maybe even talk to it a little bit. That little bit that you do every day is what grows that seed into a big tree.

That's exactly what you're doing right now. You've just planted your seed to grow your real estate business. That seed needs you to water it a little bit every day.

If you forget about your business one day, then responsibilities, distractions and excuses pile up. If you let up even one day, the following day will feel twice as hard to get going.

After a while, the whole business adventure that you so wanted is gone. Therefore, I encourage you to do a little bit every day.

In conclusion, I want to welcome you to the team. This is just the first step to your journey with us. With my training and education, I have so much more to give you.

This book is just the beginning. There are so many other things that we do with software and technology, live events, other books, and video trainings.

I can help you, as a real estate investor, not only get underway but get to the next level. This is not the old method of real estate business. There are so many new things for you to learn.

This book is to give you direction and guidance. It is a preview before we start working with you on a more advanced level.

Also, I encourage you to check out our free coaching videos at www.REISuccessCoaching.com/freevideos.

See what we're all about and get to know us a little bit better. Visit my blog site!

We're also on Facebook, Twitter, MySpace, and LinkedIn. www.FaceBook.com/RealEstateInvestingReiSuccessTips you can get to the rest here.

You can even call our office at 1-866-592-2429, extension 1 and find out more about us.

Watch for our live events. You can experience what we do and interact with us. Participating in live events will allow you network with like-minded real estate investors and really expand your business model.

We would actually love to partner with you on your deals. If you find a deal and bring it to us, you can fill out a deal submission form and send it to us. We have buyers already.

We'll analyze the deal and review it for you and even send it to our buyers. If there's a $20,000 profit, we'll cut you a check for $10,000. It's a great way to get your business started. We're here to support and help you get to the next level.

It's been my pleasure giving you this training, and I look forward to seeing you at a live event in the near future. I want to see your business model grow and hear your success testimonial.

We love to see our students advance to a whole new lifestyle by simply following our program to reach their goals and ambition for life.

I hope that you implement what you've learned here! Take all this into consideration and open your mind to a new way of building wealth. Real estate is the key for you to get rich now.

It is like having the missing piece to your puzzle. We can help you get to the next level, and we can do it together. If you are looking for more advance training then please reach out to us and we can show you how our students are making huge profits in today market.

Looking forward in talking with you,

Zack Childress

www.Co-Wholesaling.com/ebookbonus

Don't Forget to Claim Your Free Bonus That Came with this Book

My Co-Wholesaling Blueprint ($197.00 Value)

The Step by Step Process to Make $5000 in 7 Days

Without any Experience, Cash, or Credit

Download at:

www.Co-Wholesaling.com/ebookbonus

Made in the USA
Middletown, DE
17 February 2017